Labor, Politics, and OUR Economy

What they do not want you to know!

First Edition

By Ron Davis

CONTENTS

Foreword

Introduction:

Not What You Thought it Was

Conclusion:
Really Fixing the Problem

Foreword

The USA is the greatest country on earth, but today it is fighting an unseen war. This is a war not of violence, but of economics. At its center are the independent business owners, skilled tradesmen, and entrepreneurs on which the health of our nation depends. I am writing this book for all of these people engaged in this ongoing struggle for our future, and with the hopes that those who do not yet understand it will.

This book addresses the role of unions in our economy. It does not do so in a positive light. Nothing said here is meant to demean union members, but the unions cannot undo what they have done to our economy and to themselves.

I am no doubt passionate about this topic. My opinion on it will be clear enough. But arguments require proof over opinion, and I have tried to include all the facts as best as they could be found. If I do not include enough positive, third-party studies in favor of unions it is simply because they could not be found. Still, I encourage everyone who reads this book to find the facts for themselves. If you do so, I am sure that you will discover that the vast majority of what is said in what follows holds true... no matter from which side of the issue you originally began.

If you have any other problems with this book or my opinions then all I can say is that I am sorry, but it is time that we look at the issue directly and admit where the true danger to our economy lies.

And for the thousands of labor attorneys who might like to sue me after reading this, just remember... this book is a work of fiction with exception of all of the facts. I describe the basics in this book and in no way claim to be a legal expert. I would advise any employer to contact a lawyer specializing in labor law, and employees to contact the appropriate government office when dealing with unionism.

Finally, before we begin, I want you to ask yourselves a simple question:

What percentage of US workers do you think belong to unions in the first place?

Ron Davis

March 2009

Introduction

Not What You Thought it Was

Question: *What percentage of US workers belong to*
unions?

Answer: 12.1% (Bureau of Labor Statistics, January
2008)

A little over twelve percent of American workers belong to
unions. That's all. If you're like me, it's probably not what
you guessed.

There are some other interesting facts about unions as well.
You might not have realized that almost 30% of all union
workers live in one of two states: California and New York.
Nearly half of all the union workers live in one of six states:
California, New York, Illinois, Michigan, Pennsylvania, and
New Jersey.

No one trade is entirely unionized. On a national average,
government workers have the highest percentage of union
membership at 41.8%. Construction, by way of contrast, is
only 13.9%.

Many of us have long been taught or believed that the unions our grandfathers fought for came about as the result of a noble cause: the protection of workers' safety and appropriate rights as well as to ensure a high level of quality and skill on the job. We are enthralled with the "story" of Jimmy Hoffa and are touched by movies that portray the working man's struggle.

But while this book is not about was or was not needed 100 years ago in our country, it's worth it to take a look at how this history really started.

Back in the depression era when unions gained in popularity, almost 25% of our country was unemployed. Government programs like food stamps, unemployment pay, and Medicaid did not exist. The unemployed had nothing and were virtually left to starve.

The few people that did have a job were very fortunate. In fact, they were happy to have any job when so many people had none.

But for some this wasn't good enough. In their endeavor to obtain easier work rules and higher pay, they resorted to tactics usually associated with criminals: walking off of the job to stop productivity (*Blackmail*), surrounding a business to prevent deliveries (*Holding Hostage*), destroying company property (*Vandalism*), and harassing, beating, and even sometimes killing employees hired to replace them (*Harassment, Assault, etc.*).

Due to the already high unemployment rate, politicians were afraid of further negative labor-related publicity and offered very little assistance to businesses in preventing these crimes. But even if the complaints of some of these workers were legitimate, the tactics used in the early days of union organizing were not. Union organizers were not doing this to a foreign country, they were doing it to other Americans. Their actions contradict the very principles on which our society is based: freedom, personal responsibility, and appropriate rewards for one's own efforts and risks. What about the company that was opened by someone who took the risk and put in the effort and sweat to make something large enough to employ other people in the first place? What about the American replacement workers that were elated not to be unemployed? Did those who harassed them ever consider their rights finally to have a chance to feed their families or clothe their children? What happened to their rights in this great country?

We all want more. I would like more money and less work. But instead of picking up a baseball bat and threatening my employer and the customers, the more civil thing to do would be look for another job or start my own business if I'm unhappy with where I am. That possibility is what America stands for; it's what makes us who we are.

Today unions are nothing more than a cancer on our economic system. Their singular goal is increasing the power and fortunes of their leaders. And today's primary target is YOU, the taxpayer! Union leaders figured out over the years that politics is a more powerful tool than the strong-arm tactics that gave them their start. Government spends more money than anyone else in this country and unions spend endless amounts of time and countless dollars ensuring that the laws protect and help expand their control over the workforce and the economy through both private and taxpayer-funded projects.

The purpose of this book is to educate. To show how as the result of union actions, businesses with as little as 2 employees are strangled out of existence, countless billions of taxpayers' dollars get squandered, companies are forced to send jobs overseas, and politicians put the needs of a few deep-pocketed union leaders and lobbyists over taxpayers.

I will include common sense, 3rd party studies, statistics, and most likely some opinion. Pay attention to their replies about this book because most if not all union arguments seem to be based on "we say", "we show", "we promise", or someone we hired said.

Chapter 1

Union Make Up and Tactics

Unions evolved out of Guilds. Guilds were organizations in which "membership was by profession or craft, and the primary function was to establish local control over that profession or craft by setting standards of workmanship and price, by protecting the business from competition, and by establishing status in society for members of the guild." (www.infoplease.com)

Today's unions, much like these older guilds, have the primary agenda of Money and Power. Hidden behind their propaganda of pride, unity, and fairness lies their true goal of competition elimination and control.

Of course, this is not how many unions and their advocates portray themselves. If you look at some of the web sites that promote a positive view of union history, it appears as if unions are the sole reason we no longer allow indentured servitude, slavery, or child labor. Some even go so far as to take credit for starting the revolutionary and civil wars! (www.kentlaw.edu/ilhs/curricul.htm#2)

But the heart of unionism is far from the true spirit of America. To best understand the core ideology of unions, one would do well to look up the definition of Communism. You will find them strangely similar.

The Communist ideal of "sharing the wealth" has never worked in practice. Though we may all be human beings, every single person on this planet is different from the next: we do not work, think, or have the exact same ambitions. Some people will naturally put in more or less effort than others. And the very second that one person realizes that the person next to them is putting in less effort but doing the same job for the same paycheck, the theory of equal sharing goes in the toilet.

Here is a breakdown of union types and examples of their power among us and themselves:

Workers at a single company can form their own union, but the power of such a union is limited as it exists only within their own group. If a strike or bargaining issue comes up they may not have much support from other unions.

For this reason, smaller unions will band together to form "local" unions. Since they incorporate more members, they tend to have greater recognition and thus more influence over local politics.

National Unions are formed out of many smaller local unions from all over the US. Membership, dues and political power are correspondingly increased.

Union Associations form when several National and even local unions agree to work together. Now this is not one union that directly represents workers but is more like a club that other unions join to increase their power collectively. These unions combined consist of thousands of voting employees and dues paying members. Such a large concentration of resources equals tremendous political power.

The presidents and other executives of most unions are elected by the union members. These are high power, high profile, well-paid positions and, as we all know, powerful elected positions are not obtained by just anyone. Realistically, a low-level union worker would have about as much chance being elected president of the national union as they would Governor of the State.

From this point, the operation of a large union is not that different from the operation of any other business. Unions may say that their goals are based solely on the betterment of the worker, but in practice the aim of union leaders is to keep dues money flowing and to be re-elected to that high paying, powerful job.

Union officials and support staff (paid jobs for running the union itself) are supported by union dues and administration fees attached to some benefits. So to keep those jobs, the primary aim of union employees has always been on maintaining and increasing union dues. The only ways to increase dues are:

1. Charge existing members more. This would not be popular or help get anyone re-elected.

2. Increase membership. More membership equals more dues but depends on more work being available.

3. Make more work. More work means more hours, more members, and better morale. It also makes re-election more promising.

Since unions do not directly control the amount of work available in the economy, the primary way unions make more work is to insure that what work is available is done by unionized workers. So for a union to actually get more work they need to eliminate or absorb competition. They do this through a number of strategies: by pressuring workers at non-unionized companies to join the union, by pressuring union companies and others not to buy or solicit services from independent companies, by pressuring policy makers lobbying to pass laws that give them an unfair advantage (union only policies, prevailing wage rules, etc.).

Unions use different strategies to gain a foothold in an existing company or business depending on its size. A union will look at a large company and see the potential of several thousand new dues-paying members, so they will continuously attempt to organize that company's employees. But they look at a smaller company in a completely different way. A union will sometimes attempt to organize a small company to bring a small additional amount of work into the union domain. But they equally know that the added expense of fighting or becoming union will often put a small company out of business. This means that competition has either been eliminated or absorbed into their ranks and that their chances of securing work for larger union companies is more likely.

The newly unionized employees from one of these small, now closed, companies are often left in a difficult position. They must wait and see if the union will have work for them somewhere else, but often find that they are now at the wrong end of a waiting list that has many existing union members waiting ahead of them.

Once established, unions will use a variety of tactics to maintain power and control:

1. **Strike.** We all know this one. When a contract is up for negotiation and the two sides cannot come to an

agreement, the union will demand that workers strike and walk off of the job.

2. **Strike Picket.** This is when striking employees stand in front of their employers business and hold signs to let all other unions and sympathetic people know that there is a labor issue. The aim of the picket is to keep others from working, soliciting, delivering, or otherwise supporting the employer during the strike. This is often called the "line," like a line drawn in the sand between 2 rivals. No union employee (even if they are not part of the same union or employed by the same employer) is supposed to cross that line. Temporary workers or customers who want to go to the business and have to cross the line or walk past the striking picketers are often targets of harassment. Any union employee of the business that goes to work without permission could be removed from the union or fined.

3. **Discriminatory hiring practice complaints.** Union employees apply for work in an independent shop. If union people are not hired then a discrimination complaint is filed with the government. It is illegal to not hire someone based on union status, so the burden and expense falls on the company to defend against any charges that arise.

4. **Salting.** The union will have a union employee covertly hired at an independent company or enrolled at an independent training facility. This person is commonly called a "salt". This person's sole function is to cause disharmony among the employees or students with the goal of organizing a pro union vote. Often if the person does not see the possibility of organizing the employees then they do as little work as possible until being fired.

The union may then file discrimination charges against the employer or facility over the firing.

5. **Scaling.** This is where the union offers employees of an independent company the opportunity to join the union if they quit, causing immediate employee shortages for the company. For example, when our own company was awarded a large, high-profile project the union tried scaling employees. Every employee that had ever applied to the union apprenticeship program was "coincidently" notified after the start of the job that they had been accepted into the program. The catch: if they agreed to join the union they had to quit working for us, hoping to leave us shorthanded and hinder our ability to complete the job. It did not. In fact, 50% of the employees that did take the offer came back to work for us at a later date.

6. **Honey.** This is the oldest form of takeover. A union official finds employees and tells them benefits of joining the union, omitting several key issues unless the employee is educated enough to know the right questions. For example, the union representative told my employees that they could get paid while laid off, but the real story was that the employees could pay into a fund that would reimburse them when laid off up to a certain amount depending on how much they paid into it. Our employees knew that their paychecks were often more than those of union employees after all the deductions, and that they already received benefits like paid holidays, paid vacation, and company paid health insurance on par with those of unions. They also knew that they would be on the bottom of the hiring hall list and that people were already waiting for work. But foremost they were smart enough to realize that all of the work we did get was because we were independent,

and going union would mean that the company would instantly have fewer customers and less work.

7. **Informational Picket.** This is the one you see most often on construction sites. Though they look similar (guys standing around with signs or umbrellas), by law they are not the same. An informational picket is allowed for a union to protest that workers are being employed at less than the "prevailing wage". While this is legally supposed to do nothing other than inform people, it is set up and carried out to obtain the same results as a strike picket, i.e., "Do not support this company!".

8. **Informational Picket Observer.** Since the law allowing dual gates (one entrance for union workers and one for everyone else) was passed forcing informational picketers to stand at only the designated non-union gate that is usually placed in the most hidden or least effective location, the observer was invented. An Observer (who looks a lot like a picketer) is allowed to stand at any location including the union gate but is not supposed to say anything to prevent someone from entering the site. The observers supposed function is to ensure that only union people enter through the union gate.

9. **Handbills.** This is where a union person will stand outside of a business after they are open (sometimes for months) and hand out pamphlets stating that the business used substandard labor during construction. Who determined that your labor was substandard? They did. What defines "substandard" for them? Not belonging to their union, of course!

10. **Advertising.** Unions will buy TV, Radio, Newspaper ads, and Billboards to let people know that a business

uses independent labor. For example, we did a large job for a retail clothing store and a union organization rented a large billboard on the highway asking people not to go to the store because they used out-of-state workers (trying to imply "illegal aliens"). In the end, the store did 20% more in sales than projected and was appreciative of the free advertising they received.

11. **Complaint Filing.** The US Department of Labor (DOL), National Labor Relations Board (NLRB), etc., regulate labor laws and impose heavy fines for violations. The cost of filing a governmental complaint is negligible, but the potential cost to a company is devastating. Government agencies do not care if the company has 2 employees or 2000. They follow the exact the same procedures, apply the same fines and penalties, regardless of size.

12. **Propaganda.** Unions are constantly pummeling their members and the public with pro-union information that exaggerates the benefits of membership but disregards the costs.

13. **Politics.** Union lobbying is big business. Unions heavily invest in politics to ensure that laws are passed or contracts awarded that favor unions.

14. The old fashioned **Jimmy Hoffa** tactics are rarely proven but in my opinion still occasionally used today.

15. **Project funding.** Unions will at times supplement a percentage of union contractor's bids so that they can outbid independent companies if they do not want them to have the work.

16. **Work Harmony clauses.** Unions will often convince landlords to include a work harmony clause in lease agreements. They use this to prevent independents from

working on commercial properties because the potential of the union putting up a picket or hand billing would disrupt tenants and create disharmony. But from my understanding the National Labor Relations Board (NLRB) does not allow union pickets to disturb or hinder the operation of other businesses and would require the union to stop.

Unions have other tactics at their disposal, but these are the backbone of the arsenal they use to eliminate independent companies and control already unionized ones.

One newer tactic that unions are trying to develop *at this very moment* deserves special attention and concern (if it has become law before you read this, I AM SORRY!). This is the Card Check Law, currently part of something called the "Employee Free Choice Act" or some other such nonsense.

They call it "free choice" because currently employers have a few days to communicate with their employees before a union vote that is taken publicly. When I say publicly I mean the union, federal representatives, and the business representatives are there at the time of the vote but no one knows what anyone is voting, just like our government elections. But unions contend that this allows employers to threaten employees.

The Card Check Law would only require the union to gather over 50% of employees signatures on cards over a 6 month period for a workplace to become unionized. If this is accomplished, then it is a done deal. No vote, no viewpoints of the employer (who may not even know signatures are being gathered), no government agency present when the cards are signed, etc.

Business owners argue that besides not being able to voice their opinions to employees, cards could be signed without the employees realization of what they were signing or the impact of their decision. Not to mention that the only people who know what circumstances the card was signed under are the union representatives and the employee. Was the employee intoxicated, bribed, threatened, or misled into signing the card? No one would ever know.

You might say "Well, that's ridiculous and lawmakers would never let that pass."

You would be wrong.

But that is for another chapter…

Chapter 2

To Be or not To Be Union

A union is a group of workers who agree to have an elected person represent and negotiate employment terms on their behalf. Employees within a trade are not required to join the larger, already established unions representing their trade. Employees are always free to start their own separate unions. The federal government will recognize these unions, but the larger unions may not.

The US Department of Labor (DOL) governs this area and will be more than happy to let you know that your employees have the right to form or join a union.

There are no special qualifications or training required to be union. Legally any company with 2 or more employees can be forced into a union with 50% + 1 employee votes. But to say that a simple majority of employees are required to unionize a company is misleading. A number of employees may be exempt from the count and vote. For example, say you have 11 employees total but 6 of them are relatives, 2 are office employees, and 1 is a job foreman in a management position. This could leave as little as 2 vote eligible employees to determine the union status and future of your business. If those two employees decide to vote for the union, then according to DOL rules, your company is now in full union negotiations.

At this stage a small company forced to spend money on lawyers and facing the potential of government fines could easily be put out of business. By the same token, having higher cost due to the labor union could make them non competitive and put them out of business as well. Oh, by the way, if the company does make it through the election and expense still in business without being union, then the unions can just start the process all over again later. Thanks to unions, small businesses face a never-ending, lose-lose battle.

Now you may be sitting there pondering about how hard you've always heard it is to get into the union and wondering why I write like it is the easiest thing in the world. Well, the explanation is a little of both, but the end result is always a disadvantage to business.

Most large unions only accept new members if work is available and no current members are laid off and waiting for work. The process of getting new members in this case is more like being part of a "friends and family" plan. The other way would be to already have a job in a field that the union you would like to get into covers, see if they are even interested in unionizing your company, and then convince 50% +1 of your fellow workers to form a union.

Unions are all separate entities just like businesses, and just because you work for one does not mean that you can work for another or that they even like yours. For example, imagine that you start a union at work. Call it "Lollypop Local 4". Well, "Lollypop Local 3" may already exist in your area and when you ask them to sign an agreement with your newly formed union they may say "ok" or, just as likely, they may say "NO, and we do not recognize *your* union".

Recognize our union? What does this mean, you ask? To continue, imagine Lollypop Local 3 has agreements with "Soda Local 37," "Chocolate Local 28," and "Ice Cream Local 7." These locals all provide services to THE BIG STORE. Now, if your Lollypop Local 4 wants to provide services at THE BIG STORE and Lollypop Local 3 and the others hear about it, they'll just tell THE BIG STORE that *they* do not recognize your union and that if the store uses your services (that are in direct competition with them) they will all picket the store! And this, despite the fact that the federal government itself has already recognized your union!

OOPS! You may be "union," but you have about the same chance of selling at THE BIG STORE as an independent.

What happened to that propaganda about "brotherhood, solidarity, and sticking together" we have heard so much about? The fact is that established unions only care about themselves. Lollypop Local 3 only cares that everyone uses their services; union status is irrelevant. They view other unions in the same craft as being as big an enemy as an independent. Why? HELLO, because they are in it for Money and Power! Period.

Next time you hear a union complaining that someone is not union, please replace that with what they really mean: that someone is not in *our* union.

This fact alone is one of the chief reasons why unions almost always have a negative impact on employee morale and overall business production. Here are some examples how:

Unions lower incentives to work harder and increase your skills. Since a union is closer to communism than democracy, everyone is equal with equal pay and seniority often trumps skill. You might be doing twice as much work as the other guy

29

but at the end of the week your paychecks are identical, so you will slow down; the guy that does less than you gets a promotion not because he is more skilled, but because he has been doing it longer than you have.

Unions lower overall productivity. For example, workers can get fined by the union because they cut a piece of wood they needed to finish a task and that was "someone else's" job. Or often foremen scold those who work too fast because that much production will be expected the next time, or because they want the job to drag out for more hours. [One of our employees that had been scaled off of our company told his brother-in-law who still worked for us this story: His union was called into a big meeting and told that some very large national companies threatened that if they did not produce as much work as their independent counterparts used in other parts of the country they would be forced to bring in independent companies to do the work. So he went into work the next day and started working harder, really knocking out some work, until his foreman told him that if he did not slow down he would be sent back to the hall.]

Unions do not improve a worker's chances of work. I have heard countless stories about how unions have left employees high and dry. Most people, especially the union workers, do not fully realize that they work for the company and belong to the union. Your employer may not stay in business due to the added cost of unions or may send your job to a plant somewhere else. Unemployed is still unemployed even if you're union. Or you might find yourself sitting on the bench for weeks while some slow derelicts keep getting sent to work before you due to seniority. And unions will often have what they call "books". Book 1 may include all union members that became members due to the friends and family plan; Book 2 may include all of the union members that were scaled off of a competing company; and Book 3 could be for all union members that became members by voting in a company. The number or breakdown of books could be as unlimited as the imagination, but job placement may be based on what book you are in. If you are out of work and are from a voted in company, most likely they will offer any available jobs to everyone in book 1 first, then book 2, before ever getting to book 3 and your being sent to work.

Unions do not care about the businesses that provide jobs in the first place. I was on a jobsite and the construction supervisor told a member of a particular trade union that if they did not work faster or get more people on the job to catch up with the schedule, then his company would sue the contractor out of business. The union workers reply was: "Go ahead and sue them, the union will just send me to work for someone else." How effective or economical is it when union employees tell their employers I do not have to, or I do not care; when doing as little as required is considered a good days work, or when employees have no company pride? The answer is simple: not very.

Our world is getting smaller everyday and economics drives every company and employee. But remember that if you force a company to pay an employee too much and thereby raise prices, the company's competitor from next door or the next country is going to take the customers and there will be no work for you to get paid more to do.

Why are over 85% of US workers not in a union? BECAUSE THEY DO NOT WANT TO BE!

Chapter 3

Unions and Employee Skills

"Training" and "skill" are very wide terms. They are not always interchangeable. If it takes me 200 hours to train a person to bolt on a wheel and 400 hours to train a monkey to do the same thing, does that mean the monkey has more training?

Unions would like you to believe that their members are very well-trained individuals, but trained in what? And how productive were all of those training hours?

Unions base a large amount of their claims to usefulness on their training, but tend to neglect mentioning several key points. For instance, all of our employees were trained and certified on the installation of a particular system. The training was provided by the manufacturer (a Fortune 500 company) and the training class consisted of employees sent in by both union and independent companies. We were all in the same class, we all received the same instruction and materials, and after 2 days of training, we all received the same certification.

So my point is that most of what goes by the name "Union Training" is realistically company-provided training and could probably be accomplished by replacement workers in a couple of weeks.

Union apprentice training is something different, and in trades that require an apprentice program it is most likely that independent workers already have it.

What? Well, yes, the unions offer apprentice programs but so do many independent companies, trade schools, and trade organizations. And, yes, independents have Department of Labor approved apprentice training courses. You also have to keep in mind that all apprenticeship programs consist of mostly bookwork and very little class time hands on learning. While all apprenticeship programs require thousands of hours of On-the-Job Training (OJT), such training is not rigorously governed and primarily consists of an employer simply reporting hours worked.

You can debate whether one system of training is better than another, but most of the general population assumes a "journeyman" in a particular field has been through an apprentice training course first, but that is not always true.

While the issue can be very confusing, I will try and point out several ways that someone can become "classified as a Journeyman".

1. Complete the requirements of a DOL approved training course.

2. On a prevailing wage project (described in further detail later) the DOL determines that anyone not currently enrolled in an approved apprentice class is considered a Journeyman. So, in this case, no experience and no training class = Journeyman.

3. Some municipalities require proof of experience and testing to be considered a Journeyman and union or independent status is irrelevant.

4. Some people just say they are.

5. People who have not taken any apprentice course are
    sometimes classified as journeymen by unions in an
    effort to organize a company.

Not all union journeymen, in short, have been through an
approved apprentice training course. In fact, I would wager that
if they ever made it known how many of their "journeymen"
have actually been through a DOL approved course it would be
a lower percentage than many would expect.

It also needs to be kept in mind that just because the employees
of a company vote to unionize, this does not mean that the
company is instantly better or that the employees wake up more
skilled. When a union takes over a company there is no change
in company policy with the exception of how it compensates its
employees. Existing employees are not replaced or instantly re-
trained. It is the exact same company, only now with a labor
agreement between the company and its employees.

Unions have little to no influence over training. Skill and safety
training may be provided by the union, but is more often left up
to the company. Even with DOL programs, the majority of the
required training is done on the job. You have to get it out of
your head that the union teaches the people how to run a
factory's machines or to put washer A into slot B. They do not.

Do you realize that if two identical houses were built next to
each other and one was built union and one was not, their
appraisal value would be the same? If the simple fact of having
union workers contributed to value in any significant way, then
how could this be the case?

Did you know that municipalities that require license, permits,
bonds, and inspections require the same from independent and

union contractors? Local inspections and inspectors are the same for both and it is illegal to discriminate between them.

In reality, union status alone matters little. What does matter, what *only* matters, is experience, skill, and merit.

Unfortunately today -- due to inner work rules, policy, and work ethics -- several unions are quickly changing the old perception of union "quality and skill" into "slow, lazy, and expensive".

Unions have no one to blame but themselves.

Chapter 4

Unions and Business

All large businesses started off as smaller businesses, and no one walks around with a hat that we all pull a number out of to see if we are awarded a successful business. A successful business requires hard work, sacrifice, skill, and ambition.

The United States is the greatest country on earth because we can make our own decisions and have the right to stick our necks out and make something for ourselves. But this is not to say that business here doesn't face obstacles. The primary barriers to business success are finances, customers, taxes, legal issues, and unions.

I own a small company in the commercial construction industry that employs anywhere between 3 and 10 people depending on the work available. The company started out with 1 employee, ME, but even now I personally do all of the bidding, billing, hiring, firing, payroll, collections, insurance, and general office work to make the business run. I file the taxes, obtain the permits, order major materials, check jobs in progress, deal with work issues, deal with customer issues, deal with employee issues, and at times still work on jobs.

I make decent money and have equal opportunity to make millions or go bankrupt. But doing the actual work is the easiest part of my business. On top of the job itself, I have to find customers, find ones willing to use an independent contractor, bid against other companies, and hope that once the work is complete that my customer pays in a timely fashion (they rarely do!). In addition to all of this, I have to fight off the union the entire time, not because the employees want to be union but because the unions do not want us to have the work.

When it comes to making a living, we all have the same choices in life: do nothing, work for others, or work for ourselves. I would like to do nothing, but it does not pay well; working for others paid better, but would take a very long time to achieve my goals. So I chose to work for myself, to stick my own neck out to have a chance to achieve the financial stability I desired.

In the end, businesses and workers are motivated by the same desires. A worker goes to work to earn as much money as they can; a business is in business to make as much money as it can. But this doesn't mean that they are the same. The difference between the two is risk. I might take a risk and end up losing money on a job. But the workers get paid regardless. Unions try to blur this line and believe that just because a business makes money, the union employees deserve part of it while taking none of the risk.

Unions went from promising a livable wage and safe working environment to judging an employer's profit margin and demanding that workers be treated like shareholders. Only unlike shareholders, their wages never go down if profits fall off.

Unions complain about jobs going out of the country and blame everyone but themselves for it. The truth is that large companies have stockholders and competition and need to do whatever is necessary to remain competitive and make the stockholders money. That is the way business works no matter how you look at it.

With technology the world has become much smaller. Competition for a US based company is no longer just other US based companies. And with our current global economy you really have no idea who owns what or often where something was originally produced. People need to understand that today "MADE in the USA" could mean assembled in the US from parts produced in another country. Or that a US based company's major stockholders are foreign companies or citizens. Products entirely made in the US by solely US owned companies are few and far between.

Big business today is multinational. Stockholder Jimmy from Germany could care less where the TV company he owns stock in makes the TVs or if they are union, only that his stock goes up in value (p.s. the US no longer has any large TV manufacturers). Companies in this sense really have no patriotic duty to any one country, only the stock holders.

ANY company that hopes to survive has to look first at the competition. This tells them about how much they can charge for their finished product. Next they have to figure out how much it is going to cost to make the product. This is determined by figuring out everything from materials to labor to administrative costs, etc.. Finally they have to determine if a profit can be made. Spending $5 to make a corndog that everyone else makes for $1 would not be a good business decision and truthfully neither would making them for the same $1 everyone else does. To have half a chance to survive you will have to make better corndogs and make them for only $.95 cents.

How would you like it if you bought $1000 worth of stock in a cup making company and your neighbor bought $1000 dollars worth of stock in a different cup making company and his stock went up and yours went down? You probably won't care much about union labor or foreign status, only your loss and the up and down just like everyone else. And like most investors if your neighbor's keeps going up then you will most likely sell your stock and buy his.

Competition and the search for the best value, in other words, guide the decision making of both companies and individuals. Unfortunately, because of a number of factors, this has spelled trouble for US producers and manufacturers. Today our imports exceed our exports by about $677 billion dollars a year. I am not a math expert, but even I can figure out that selling $1 trillion dollars worth of stuff to other countries and buying $1.7 trillion dollars worth of stuff from those countries every year cannot be a good thing. Today we are even lucky if all of that foreign made stuff we buy is bought out of a US owned store!

Every one of those dollars represents a lost opportunity for profit, a lost job, and, most important, lost independence. And a majority of this loss can be blamed on a single source: unions.

Even a well-established US based company has to look at labor cost. Over the years while union contracts have given employees a little more of this and a little more of that, they have become less and less flexible. While competitive circumstances change and worsen, labor leaders refuse to budge.

Currently we are having major trouble with the automakers. Their demise would mean massive unemployment and seriously hurt our economy. One of the main reasons (if not the only reason) are the union employees. Besides the fact that someone some time ago agreed that it would be a good idea to pay employees while not working, over the years increased union pay, work rules and benefits have made labor costs uncompetitive with their foreign counterparts. When faced with bankruptcy the union was asked to reduce their pay to match the UNION foreign car plants in the UNITED STATES. They said NO!

What many do not realize is that there are only two ways to get the union pay back in line with the competition:

1. Declare bankruptcy – This would void all union contracts but could also void pensions and have further economic impact on smaller suppliers and dealers. Plus, union employees would be flooding the unemployment office costing billions in unemployment benefits.

2. Have the Federal Government step in – Not only with federal loans, but by forcing the auto unions to accept a working agreement that would allow the auto makers to compete with their foreign counterparts and actually start making a profit.

Unions would like you to believe that all jobs leaving our country are being done for $1 a day, by child labor, in horrendous circumstances. But in reality the vast number of foreign workers have benefited from their jobs. You can find instances of child labor or extremely low pay by shady companies anywhere, but they are the exception and not the rule.

Foreign workers doing those jobs are just like you and me. They just easily took the jobs away from us by working for less. You may be outraged that you lost your job costing the company $70 per hour (if $70 per hour was not on your check you better ask the union where it went) to some guy 3,000 miles away, but I can assure you he is happier than heck to have the job even if you do not think he is being paid enough.

It is a shame to think that burdensome labor rules and costs have encouraged companies to determine that spending billions of dollars to build plants in 3rd world countries that could be taken by the government at any time, train new workers, deal with language barriers, long commutes, and pay more for shipping to and from the US was a good business decision. We can blame ourselves for allowing unions to do this.

You know Aunt Sally may be a union worker making $70 per hour bolting on that wheel the machine holds up for her when she is actually required to be at work, but her union is going to force the company to a point that eventually some person in a place like Mexico has Sally's job for $20 per hour and she is living with you because she has no job! Not only that, since our laws make it hard for the company to pay Sally less or get rid of her and offer the job to another American, that job is just gone. Now less people are coming into the place *you* work and *your* job may soon be gone too.

The US population is about 306 million people. The world population is about 6.75 billion (that's about 22 times our population). Those other 6.44 billion people want jobs and money just like we do. And they could care less about our labor laws or unions.

Any successful business relies on skilled, well-trained employees who have a sense of company pride. You are more successful when poor performing employees can be weeded out and skilled, dedicated employees can be rewarded or promoted for their work.

But unions prevent this. When a union can tell an employer who to hire, who to promote, when to work, how much to work, and require excessive pay to do ordinary skilled work the outcome is failure.

Fortunately unions are becoming obsolete, but we need to be proactive in ensuring that they do not cause our economy any more harm than they have already.

Make companies you invest in be conscious of spending and do not simply bow down to union threats. You will find that most company leaders are not educated on many union issues and simply cave in. For example, we were awarded a contract for work on several retail cellular stores on a Thursday and by Friday the contract was taken away because an alderman called the corporate office and told them that they better use union labor. The president of the cell company decided that he did not want negative publicity in a new market so ordered all work to be union. The General Contractor and members of the company pointed out that the alderman was not even from an area getting a store, that union construction companies in the area were required to use a type of phone service they did not offer, and that the estimated cost increase would be about $300,000. But the work went union anyway, wasting investors' money.

What would have happened in the above scenario if the project had gone to independent contractors? Well, the company would have saved $300,000 for starters. But the possibilities are that the unions would have put up informational pickets trying to slow the projects down, put the company on their do not solicit list, and paid for some negative advertisement. Or not, we will never know.

The cost to investors, however, is clear. In one case, we were awarded a job remodeling an auto parts store that was part of a large national chain. The union noticed us working and called the corporate office threatening to picket and all of the other stuff. The corporate office decided to pay our contract to date and then hire the union to finish, basically paying for the job twice. I did not care since I made more money by not doing the job, but I also do not own stock in that company. In another case , we were working on a national wedding gown store and a union representative came in and threatened the General Contractor that if they did not fire the current company and hire a union company, they would put them on their do not solicit list. The GC laughed and replied "if you think any union member is going to tell their future wife or daughter that they cannot buy their wedding dress from here, then you are crazy. Get out." The rep left and was not heard from again.

Investors need to educate company decision makers about these union scare tactics. They need to convince decision makers not to give in. Unions cannot really do anything but threaten and put out some negative advertisement that no one pays attention to anyway. Look at Wal-Mart. I have seen more than one union worker sticker in the windows of cars in their parking lot. And unions think Wal-Mart is their number 1 enemy.

Studies show that unions drive up cost on public projects on average of 20%, but I find that union construction labor drives up the cost on private projects about 30% and that number increases with the cost of the project.

For a person trying to open a small business this cost difference could doom them before they ever open.

Here are some steps to prevent union disruption and added expense when opening a new location:

1. Never agree to a lease that requires union only labor. The Landlord wants your money and will change the requirement.
2. Clarify in your lease agreement that work harmony restrictions do not apply to construction.

3. Include in your construction contract that companies you hire are responsible for adequately staffing the project and keeping up with the construction schedule or heavy fines will be imposed. Also, clarify that labor issues are NOT exempt from the fines and labor issues are the sole responsibility of the contractor to be hired and cause for replacement. Include a clause that everyone is required to honor the dual gate system if implemented.

4. Post no trespassing signs. While union officials have the right to enter a site if their people are on site, they do not if their people are not. (Example: You hire a union plumber and an independent electrician, then the plumber's union representative can come on the job site but the electricians union cannot come inside. If they do, you can have the police take them away.)

5. Become familiar with the dual gate system. This is a legal system that is supposed to allow union workers an entrance to the job site that is for union people and their deliveries only (Gate A) and a second entrance for everyone else (Gate B). It has very specific rules governed by law and you should check with the appropriate government agency or a labor lawyer to clarify all rules. Essentially it is supposed to allow union workers to still come to work if an informational picket has been set up because informational picketers are only allowed to picket by the independent gate (Gate B), thereby ensuring that union employees are not crossing a picket line when entering through their gate (Gate A). No independent personnel or deliveries are allowed through the union gate or the dual gate system is void until it can be cleansed for 48 hours. Union people, of course, will sometimes go through either gate, but you better make sure an independent does not go through theirs!

6. Be sure that your general contractor prices independent contractors and shows you the bids. Sometimes companies will hire a general contractor to oversee a project and sometimes those contractors will only ask union contractors to bid the project so be careful.

7. Finally and most importantly... hold your ground. Unions will often try to make deals to relieve pressure that they are applying but even if you strike a deal with one, another one is waiting around the corner. (Example: A large store made a deal with the local that if they removed their picket the store would pay them (over $100,000) to set up the clothing racks and changing rooms that the store employees normally set up. They agreed and removed the picket, and then another union organization rented a billboard with negative statements about the company's choice in using independent labor anyway.)

Do not think that you will win by agreeing to a little portion of the pie. The unions will want it all. One union does not have the power to speak for the others, so they will all come to your door wanting their cut. *The best way to avoid this is to use all independent contractors.* Independents really could not care less who is walking around outside. And customers are only looking for the open sign.

Besides, the miniscule profit that you may or may not lose from other union workers who might pay attention is more than made up for in construction cost savings. As I just pointed out with Wal-Mart, in reality not all union workers are going to avoid your store anyway. I would bet that less than 5% even care and less than .1% would even remember that there was a union picket there a month later.

46

The number one way to keep your company independent is to educate your employees. There are several things that you and your employees do not understand, and if you educate them on these facts about unions they are less likely to be agreeable than when they are only told bits and pieces.

If you a worker and are asking why the CEO makes a million dollars a year and you make only $50K a year, the answer has nothing to do with "fairness". You have the same opportunity to go out and become a CEO making a million a year if you want to do what it takes to try for it (so stop crying and get to it!). Besides, if everyone did make the same amount, then that would be called "Communism" and throughout history Communism has never done very well.

Chapter 5

Prevailing Wage

At all levels of government, unions attempt to organize government workers and influence public sector spending with one goal in mind: to make sure that all taxpayer money is spent on union labor only.

It is clear enough that such influence is counterproductive. Just consider education. Education is not currently one of our brightest stars and one of the major problems is unions. Unions prevent poor quality teachers from being replaced or exceptional teachers from being rewarded. Unions also account for tremendous amounts of wasted expense in school construction cost. And we all know what it is like to deal with a government worker, but a union government worker? Enough said.

The current favorite strategy of unions and their supportive legislators is to talk about the need to "Level the Playing Field". They try to imply that this means making everything equal and fair for everyone. What this really means is making independent companies pay. Since union costs are so much higher than independent companies, unions can only compete by raising the expenses of independent companies. Instead of leveling the field between the two, unions make everyone pay more. One of the ways this is done is through "prevailing wage" rules.

Prevailing Wage

First let me clarify: "prevailing wage" in no way means 'Union Only'! You are not required to be union to work on a prevailing wage project.

The idea of a prevailing wage was conjured up as part of the Davis Bacon Act of 1931. This law states that all federally funded projects over $2,000.00 must pay workers the local prevailing wage including benefit cost and other work rules.

Now let me tell you about the Davis Bacon Act. This law was pushed into action due to a contractor bringing African American workers to New York to work on a large federally funded project. It was passed with the specific intent of preventing non-unionized, black, and immigrant laborers from competing with unionized white workers for scarce jobs during the Depression.

To get an idea of this, here are some quotes from politicians arguing for the act's passage:

Rep. John Cochran of Missouri said he had "received numerous complaints in recent months about Southern contractors employing low-paid colored mechanics getting work and bringing the employees from the South."

Alabama Rep. Clayton Allgood complained: "Reference has been made to a contractor from Alabama who went to New York with bootleg labor. This is a fact. That contractor has cheap colored labor that he transports, and he puts them in cabins, and it is labor of that sort that is in competition with white labor throughout the country."

Rep. William Upshaw complained of the "superabundance or large aggregation of negro labor," which is a real problem "you are confronted with in any community."

New York's Sen. Robert Bacon replied, "I just mentioned the fact because that was the fact in this particular case, but the same would be true if you should bring in a lot of Mexican laborers or if you brought in any non-union laborers from any other state."

Other congressmen expressed their support for the Davis-Bacon Act in ways that were more temperate. They railed against "transient labor", "cheap labor" and "cheap imported labor." AFL president William Green made it clear what his union's interests were, "Colored labor is being sought to demoralize wage rates."

So much for the "noble motives" of the unions. Such racist rhetoric suited their purpose for advancement at the time and shows that they will do anything to anyone to increase their money and power.

The Davis-Bacon Act covers a significant portion of the projects undertaken by the construction industry. Approximately 20 percent of all construction projects in the U.S. are covered by the Act, affecting more than 25 percent of all construction workers in the nation at any given time. (www.ij.org)

Prevailing wage is supposed to reflect the amount of pay local workers get in their field. For example, a plumber in California may be paid $25.00 per hour and a plumber in New York might get $27.00 per hour. So all companies doing federally funded prevailing wage work in California pay plumbers $25.00 per hour and all prevailing wage work in New York by plumbers pays $27.00 per hour.

Sounds fair? Well, yes, except that the wage determination is not determined by what all workers in an area are paid. Usually it is only determined by what the local union states that it is. So 100% of what the government states that an employee must be paid is usually determined by what less than 15% of the workers make. And usually has no investigation of the amount claimed.

This gets complicated and very expensive for the taxpayer, so I will try and explain it in general terms the best that I can.

1. The federal government agrees to pay for part of a new court house and the costs are over $2,000, so by law the Davis Bacon Act applies.

2. Both Union and Independent companies are legally allowed to bid and do the project.

3. The independent contractor looks up what the local prevailing wage is for their trade (i.e., for electricians, etc.). He knows that he and his independent competition pay about $28-32 dollars per hour plus benefits for journeymen and that union journeymen bring home about the same (believe it or not, the take home pay and benefits for my employees is about the same as for union ones, how else would we keep good employees?). But the prevailing wage rate stated by the unions is more like $52.00 per hour. How is this possible? (And it is not that simple either, sometimes the wage is stated as something like $25.00 times 1.75% plus $11.25, or some other crazy formula.)

4. So the independent contractor starts to figure out what the pay comparison is. An example might look like this.

Regular pay per hour	$28.00
Company paid Health insurance broken down hourly	$0.61
Company paid vacation broken down hourly (2 weeks per year)	$1.08
Company paid holidays broken down hourly (6 days per year)	$0.65
Total	$30.34
Listed prevailing Wage	$32.00 plus $19.80 fringe benefits = $51.80 per hour
Difference	$21.46 per hour

Now wait a minute... I know union employees' paychecks are similar to our employees', our health insurance is better than theirs, and holiday and vacation time seem to be similar, so where has that other $21.46 gone?

That is a good question and one that we all would like an answer to since the government takes the unions at face value and leaves the burden of proof to the rest of us. The union will, for example, state that their inferior health insurance cost is $2.65 per hour (with administration handling charges included) and no one ever checks! And while they are deducting that $2.65 per hour from $52 you can only deduct $0.61.

Now be really careful, because if you mess up on that deduction calculation by even $0.01 per hour and someone calls the NLRB and claims that you are not paying prevailing wages as required you will be fined an extraordinary amount. Most people I know round up to give a safe zone.

Now what about that $21.46 per hour?

5. You add $21.46 to the employees' hourly wage. And this is the part all independent workers love: their comparable wage just went up at the taxpayer's expense to $49.46 per hour plus benefits. The union employee's check will stay the same because according to the unions he always makes that amount minus deductions. (Now multiply X 10 men, X 8 hours per day, X 5 days per week, X 12 weeks. How much money did the government just waste requiring "prevailing wage" for the taxpayers in this example? About $103,000.00)

6. There are other stipulations you need to figure in because the government will also regulate pay for hours worked and apprentice to Journeyman ratio, etc. (Example: You cannot work just any 8 hours per day or any day, you have to pay more if the work is done outside the stated work hours even if the day is not over 8 hours or the week is not over 40 hours). The result is simple: more needless taxpayer expense.

Also wage rates go down for apprentices. But an apprentice has to be enrolled in a Department of Labor approved apprentice program. While there are many independent DOL approved classes, anyone who is not in one must be paid Journeyman Wages.

So here is an example of an interesting government rule: If the DOL states that you can have (1) 3rd year apprentice and (1) 1st year apprentice for every (1) Journeyman then that would sound as if they are stipulating a quality assurance, but not really. That only helps with payment, you are allowed to pay the 3rd and 1st year apprentices less than a journeymen (another formula) if they are in an approved apprentice program but if they are not in one then they are automatically considered Journeymen. So in their eyes you could have 1 journeyman and 50 new hires, but since they are not in an approved class the government only sees 51 journeymen.

Now for the biggest surprise: As an independent contractor you will find that even with the inflated labor cost and ridiculous work rules you will still underbid union contractors by an average of 20%!

Why? All of those internal work rules that the unions have been voting in over the years that are not required by the DOL. (Example: A union electrician is only required to install 100' of pipe per day, and he installs it in 3 hours and gets to go home while collecting pay for 8 hours of work.)

"Prevailing wage" is not a terrible concept in and of itself, but it has been terribly disfigured and used as a competition eliminating tool by the unions for far too long.

While the Davis Bacon Act only applies to federally funded projects, the unions have spent countless amounts of time and money trying to get State and Local governments to incorporate it into their laws.

By my own estimates, prevailing wage requirements needlessly drive up construction costs by 30% or more.

The US Chamber of Commerce claims that if the Davis Bacon Act was overturned it would reduce construction cost allowing for more needed construction projects and create an estimated 31,000 additional jobs.

Chapter 6

Project Labor Agreements

Since high union costs and burdensome work rules no longer ensure that unions receive all of the available prevailing wage work, unions had to come up with something new.

This meant it was time to once again "level the playing field". To do this, unions lobbied for the enforcement of Project Labor Agreements (or PLAs). Unions often try to imply that a PLA is the same as Prevailing Wage but it is NOT. While a PLA includes Prevailing Wage rules, as of March 2009 no federal law currently requires a PLA.

President Barack Obama signed an executive order that encourages construction projects using the recent stimulus package funds to implement PLA's but does not require it.

Union officials will attempt to have every construction project (tax paid or private) be put under a PLA. Since it is not a law they have to solicit every person in charge of every project to attempt to have it imposed. It usually happens at the local government level or school and fire boards because often they are not educated on the matter.

Project Labor Agreements have one purpose: to eliminate competition. You may say "Well, all of the union companies will be competing for the work so that's not the case." Sure they will, but with a PLA you just limited the bidding pool by over

85%. It is almost like saying you need a new car but can only look at one manufacturer's cars: they may have several different models, but you do not have the slightest idea what the other manufactures even have to offer. Hardly a way to make a wise use of resources!

Unions will state that a PLA does not require a company to be union. That may be true, but it requires everyone to follow the same burdensome and excessive union rules, to hire union labor, to basically treat existing employees as 'temporarily' union if they are even allowed to work on the project, and pay into union funds that will never be used by the existing employees. This makes an independent company effectively a union company in almost every way on that jobsite and the added cost is passed along to the customer or taxpayer.

PLA's come in various forms, but all have the basic goal of keeping the work union. The basic core of a PLA will usually state that if you agree to follow the union set guidelines they will:

1. **Ensure Work Harmony**. Meaning that one trade will not get upset because another trade is not union. (Independent contractors do not have this problem)

2. **Not Strike**. Implying that if you sign the agreement and there is a strike it will not affect *your* project. While unions can go to great lengths to make this happen it is not a guarantee. Federal law states that workers can strike no matter what the union says, and it has been well-documented that workers have striked and refused to work on projects with a PLA. For example, in June 2006, the Laborers International Union Local 6 engaged in a work stoppage on an $850 million project in Chicago, Illinois.

3. **Complete project on time.** They will not guarantee this either. Unions are notorious for being slow and most likely have several loopholes for this promise. It is also well documented that several PLA's have not been completed on time.

4. **Safety.** OSHA statistics show that union workers historically have a higher rate of fatalities than nonunion workers. There is no evidence to prove that workers are safer under PLAs. Safety and health management are the keys to safe workplaces – not PLAs.

5. **Complete project within budget.** Once again no guarantee or several loopholes. Besides the union contractors usually set the budget anyway. And once again there are several documented instances where this did not hold up.

Anecdotal evidence of PLA projects with cost overruns, such as the San Francisco Airport expansion, Seattle's Safeco Field, and Boston's Big Dig now years past the finish date and 13 Billion dollars over budget, show union-only PLAs are no protection against poor cost management and no guarantee that the alleged economic benefits of a PLA will translate into real cost savings.

6. Benefit minorities. Unions might imply that a PLA will benefit minorities, but The National Black Chamber of Commerce, Women Construction Owners and Executives, Latin Builders Association, National Association of Women Business Owners and other associations representing small, disadvantaged, minority- and women-owned businesses are publicly opposed to union-only PLAs. Local minority workers are shut out of jobs for much the same reason as most local workers: they overwhelmingly do not belong to unions.

The whole thing is basically ridiculous. To sum it up: the unions are saying that they want you to agree to eliminate independent contractors from the bidding pool (as no independent contractor needs work bad enough to agree to a PLA), and for your reward we will do our job on time (maybe), do it for what we said we would do it for (maybe), and not cause you any problems (maybe).

After all... strikes, work harmony issues, and pickets are only caused by unions in the first place!

It's funny how offering someone a job turns into "sign an agreement or we will cause you trouble, since part of the work will not do... we want it all"!

Maybe this little bit of satire will put the issue perspective for you: "If you would like to hire me and my employee to cut your grass one time, I will agree to not cause trouble or leave work as long as all other people that work at your house work for me or my brother; I will not let my employee or my brothers employee keep the FedEx driver from delivering to your house because they want another pay raise; I promise that we will be done cutting your yard within 1 month 'weather permitting'; and I further agree that it will not cost you over 1 million dollars. All you have to do is agree not to ask anyone else but my brother how much they would want to do it."

Independent studies from *The Beacon Hill Institute* at Suffolk University in Boston show projects that implement a PLA drive up costs by about 20%. Two studies on school building projects since 2004 both proved large increases in cost directly related to PLA's. The 2004 study showed an additional cost of about $30 per square foot and a later 2006 study showed an added cost of about $27 per square foot.

To put it in perspective, the last school project that our company completed was a midsized school of about 150,000 square feet. So according to the study, the cost difference of a PLA would be on average an additional $4,050,000.00 for this sized project. That is potentially four million dollars of wasted taxpayer money! Your money!

How many books, teachers, school busses, or school programs could they have paid for with $4 Million dollars?

How much would that waste alone cost me directly on my taxes?

Now think about this, how much was that last school, city hall, police station, or fire house that your town built? Did they ask for a bond or tax increase to pay for it? Did the school board or city council require it to have a PLA?

My local school had just threatened to cut after-school programs because the district could not afford them any longer, but later that same year the school board had a meeting to ask for a construction bond to build a new high school and vote on approving a PLA for the project.

They did not even have the money for construction yet and were already trying to make it a PLA project!

No wonder they did not have enough money for after school programs; they gave it all away on overpriced union agreements!

Another thing to be cautious of is that a public entity will only solicit general contractors to collect bids and perform the work. This might mean that a union General Contractor will only solicit union bids and you are left with virtually the same thing as a PLA.

Most of a PLA can be written into contract documents. This is the way it should be anyway: here is the work and if you want it you will not walk off the job no matter who is working and the project will be done within a reasonable time at the price you quoted or you agree to fines and replacement.

I bet if you wanted to hire a union plumber and carpenter with an independent electrician their unions would agree to any kind of work harmony if you said that they could not have the work unless they agreed in writing.

If you hear about your County, City, School Board, etc. voting on passing a PLA don't walk, RUN to the meeting and ask why they are wasting your money and ask for the unions 3rd party facts. The union will not have any since none favor them (at least none I can find) and because "we said so" has been working well enough up to now. If you are ignored and it passes anyway, I suggest you vote against them at the next election.

So in essence President Obama's executive order encourages project managers to increase construction cost about 20% and eliminate 85% of the eligible workers.

I think he needs a copy of this book

Chapter 7

Politics and Government

The union's number one tool is politics. Unions figured out a long time ago that passing laws works better than breaking heads.

It is much easier to force an employer to be union due to legal requirements than negotiate with them. It is easier to charge more when the government sets the wage rate at whatever you charge. And it is easier to eliminate the competition when the government will do it at no charge to you.

As I mentioned previously, this book is not to discuss what was needed 100 years ago but what is needed today. Unfortunately, politicians and news media are still acting as if it were 100 years ago.

Politicians need to be elected and even after they are elected they want to be re-elected. The two major things needed to get elected are money and votes.

Even though union voters only make up less than 15% of the votes, they are very organized. With their political propaganda, unions will tell their members who they want them to vote for. And even though the union cannot force them to vote for their candidate, they imply that their chosen candidate alone will help to ensure their continued employment.

When you see that advertisement for a political candidate that states that they are endorsed by, say, the teachers union, trust me: the teachers union did not ask all of its members who they like; they told them.

When a union official approaches a politician he will state that he represents union 'X' and that they have 3,000 members or maybe 100,000 members and that their members would like to see this or that happen or that they are for or against a bill. Here again, the union did not ask every union member how they actually felt about the issue.

Now, realistically, a politician has no idea how many of these union members really care about the issue, how many of the thousands even live in their political jurisdiction, or even how many of those that do even vote. But unfortunately he may be stuck on the number of voters originally mentioned.

And if that union belongs to a larger union coalition and a representative from the coalition goes in and states that they represent 10x the number of people that the first guy did, in reality a portion of his numbers are still from the first guy. So the total numbers of actual voters in question for that particular politician is still unknown. But in their mind that number of 5,000 just jumped to 55,000 concerned voters wanting what these two guys say, instead of whatever reality is. So even if 5 of us present state that we don't want what those 2 guys are wanting, the politician may not be thinking that 5 people do not like it and two do. He is thinking 5 people do not like it and *55,000* do!

Unions have all of their members contact information instantly available and at their disposal. At times they will ask all of their members to sign petitions, write letters (usually pre-printed and ready for signature), or call their representatives (names and contact information provided). And if 1% of 100,000 members actually respond, then that would be 1000 signatures, letters, or phone calls. Though I am sure the percentage is probably closer to 100% concerning petitions that have to be signed when the union rep is holding it in your face.

You may be thinking 1000 letters does not seem like much, given millions of voters, but you are wrong. I have seen this first hand on the state level. The most astounding thing that I observed was as little as 30 individuals calling or writing for or against a proposed law was a big deal! On one hand it was sad that so few people cared about laws being passed, but on the other I saw how easy it was for just a small number of people to make them take notice and pay attention. So 1000 would be a true frenzy of activity.

Unions will also go out and gather up members to take to a vote or meeting to show their support for or against an issue.

When a union official says "I represent 100,000 workers and 10 Billion Dollars in finances," he can meet with the President of the United States and the president will listen. He may not comply, but he will listen. Unfortunately, further down the political ladder listening often turns into blind, uneducated compliance.

As president Barak Obama said in his political memoir "The Audacity of Hope,"

"I owe those unions... When their leaders call, I do my best to call them back right away. I don't mind feeling obligated."

Here is another Executive order passed by President Obama that shows how unions use politicians to further their agenda.

Executive Order 13496 requires federal contractors to post a notice to employees of their rights under the federal labor laws.

This requirement is consistent with the policy of encouraging collective bargaining and protecting the right of workers to join unions. Executive Order 13496 also revokes former President Bush's Executive Order 13201, which had required federal contractors to post notices to their employees of the rights of the employees not to join a union and not to pay agency fees for activities unrelated to collective bargaining, contract administration, or grievance adjustment. Failure to comply with all provisions of the executive order may result in contract cancellation, termination, or suspension, and the contractor may be declared ineligible for future government contracts.

For example, if a union collects $1 every week from every member for political donations and has 5000 members, that is $260,000.00 per year gathered with the sole purpose of political donations. Since all unions have similar goals and employ similar tactics, the total amount of union money available to politicians is staggering.

But unions even became thrifty in this area. Here is a possible scenario to consider: unions realized that instead of saying, for instance, "we will contribute $20,000.00 to your election campaign if you favor our issues," it was less expensive to say "we will give $10,000.00 to your election campaign and if you do not favor our issues while elected, we will give $20,000.00 to the person running against you next time."

Unions will give heavily to a candidate if the one they are running against is anti union, or they may even donate to both candidates.

And that is all it takes for extreme political power, a couple of bucks from a few million people every week, an agreement to let a few people speak for the interests of many without really asking them first, and a good phone chain.

There are organizations that try to keep a good eye on union influence on lawmaking, like the US Chamber of Commerce, ABC, IEC, etc. but these organizations are usually supported by business owners and getting a couple hundred dollars a year from 200 employers does not equal a couple dollars every week from thousands of union workers. And even though these 200 employers may employ 5000 workers, the organization only represents the employers and often in the political world this only counts for 200 not 5000.

Today, as a general rule, Democrats are pro-union. Democrats receive a large amount of their political contributions from union organizations. I think that they are really uneducated in the matter and since it was the popular thing to do in the past, they continue to go with the flow.

Even if by some chance these politicians are only voting for the union population over the interests of the other 85%+ of us for political gain, it is because they think that too few of us realize what is going on or will bother to do anything about it.

Let me give a brief, general overview of our political system's make up:

1. Federal – Federal laws effect everyone
2. State – State laws only effect that particular state
3. Local – Local laws (County, City) only affect that particular area.
4. Boards – Make decisions in a certain area like school or fire department boards.

Each level of government tries naturally to limit the influence the others have over it. For example, the prevailing wage law covers the entire United States but is limited to projects that use federal money. So if your State was paying for a new hospital and no federal money was used, the prevailing wage law would not apply unless the State passed its own law to include it in any state funded projects, and so on. It could even be possible for your elected officials to vote in prevailing wage requirements when it is not required by law at any level.

Here is a list of positions that directly affect how tax money is spent and what labor laws are passed:

1.   President of the United States
2.   US Senator
3.   US Congressmen
4.   Governor
5.   State Senators
6.   State Representatives
7.   County Executive
8.   County Council
9.   Mayor
10.   City Council
11.   School Board
12.   Police Board
13.   Fire Department Board, etc.

Your state may have a different breakdown or terms for each position but this is the general idea. I am also sure that there are many other positions that determine how tax money is spent, but these are the major ones.

You may think that this is a lot of people to keep an eye on but I promise you that the union already is.

Take the time to see how many of your current elected officials are also union employees, keep an eye out for officials that are endorsed by several labor organizations, pay attention to warning phrases like 'pro-union,' 'level the playing field,' 'PLA or Project Labor Agreement,' 'Prevailing Wage,' 'work harmony,' 'fair wage,' etc.

Though the union term "fair pay" is about the widest anyone could come up with, who decides what that is? Is the approximately $70 per hour that the General Motors pays union workers fair, or is the approximate $30 per hour the foreign car makers pay US union labor fair?

Make a list of your local political representatives and their contact information. Take the time to call or e-mail your opinions. Information on all state and federal elected representatives can be found easily at the website: usa.gov.

Talk to your friends and neighbors about issues that pop up. Read the paper, attend city hall and school board meetings.

Always ask for 3rd party verification of union claims that they save money or perform better. And do not accept the reply of "because we say so", "we show", or "we think."

I am not asking you to complain about every union issue, just to understand it and make your own decision, to educate the people that do not understand, and to let your politicians know that you are aware of what they are doing.

In today's world there are government agencies and laws that protect the people and do everything that the unions claim that they stand for.

The important part is that you as an individual can change things. It takes effort, but far less than you might imagine. I have seen 3 people speaking reasonably change a School Board decision, 5 people change a city hall vote, and 50 cause a frenzy at the state capitol.

Give this book to someone who doesn't understand. Send a copy to your local politicians! Let them know that you understand exactly what they are doing even if they do not.

Conclusion

Really Fixing the Problem

As you read what I write in this chapter keep in mind that my ideas are just that: my ideas. They will probably even upset several of you who have agreed with me up to this point, and unions do not like any idea that does not give them omnipotent power, so they will certainly upset the unions.

But I believe that the ideas outlined below are our best chance to resolve the issues that confront us in a fair and realistic manner.

Eliminating the unions or labor laws is not a realistic goal or even a smart one. I hope you take from this book that labor unions and laws need to be kept in check; unions will eventually eliminate themselves if they keep on their current path. It is a shame because some of the basic ideas behind unions are noble, even if the way they have been enacted is wrong.

1. Unions need to promote employer loyalty more strongly. Business will survive without unions, but unions will not survive without businesses.

2. Unions need to be more flexible with hiring, firing, and promoting based more on business necessity and merit than seniority

3. Unions need to realize that company profit equals a stronger company and more work, not necessarily or immediately higher pay

4. Companies need a labor law that lets them re-negotiate their entire labor contract or replace workers if the company is in financial jeopardy (though 'financial jeopardy' would have to be carefully defined).

5. Project Labor Agreements or anything similar that limits or prevents some companies from bidding or performing work on publicly funded projects other than past experience should be outlawed (including requirements that past experience come from some type of union work or reference). After all, everyone's taxes are paying for that courthouse... so why can't I work on it unless I agree to be represented, not just by any union, but by *your* union in particular?

6. Adjust current laws back to *real* fairness for 100% of the work force.

• In 1931 legislators set an amount of $2,000.00 for the Davis Bacon Act to be imposed. Today, adjusting for inflation that would equal $28,000+. Though I would prefer the amount to be at least $100,000, let us at least update the amount, clarify that the amount is for expected labor cost only and not including material cost (Installing a generator for example could cost $100,000.00 but $80,000.00 of that is the cost of materials and only $20,000.00 is labor), and include an inflation adjustment factor.

• Change the current requirement of "2 employees" making a company eligible for a forced union vote and DOL requirements to "over 10 employees or owner consent". This way a small shop can be encouraged to grow without harassment and the owner still has the opportunity to be a union shop if they fall under the minimal requirements.

• Make it illegal for any trade union or organization to implement any type of picket, hand-billing, or effort to prevent

72

customers, workers, or deliveries from visiting the site of a company that employs 10 or fewer people.

• Make it illegal for a trade union or organization to implement any type of picket, hand-billing, or effort to prevent customers, workers, or deliveries from visiting the site of a company whose employees belong to any DOL recognized labor union.

• Set the prevailing wage at a fixed minimum amount for all construction personnel and trades for each State and major city based on real average data like tax returns not union calculated pay scale. Currently taxpayers are paying wages that have absurd fringe benefit amounts that need to be brought back into reality. For example: New York County New York an electrician makes $46.00 per hour plus $34.81 per hour in "fringe benefits". What are those fringe benefits that every taxpayer in the US is paying for? Has anyone bothered to check? In Los Angeles County California the electrician's pay scale is $35.95 plus "fringe benefits" of 3%+$17.72 (I talked about these formulas earlier) equaling about $18.80 in fringe benefits. Now why are the fringe benefits we are all paying for almost twice as much in New York compared to California and why is the base pay $10 per hour different? The cost of living is in fact slightly higher in California than New York so why are taxpayers paying a New York Electrician about $26.06 per hour more than one in Los Angeles? Because the current system is FLAWED!

• Set work hours on prevailing wage work at straight time: 8 hours per day, 40 hours per week. Overtime: over 8 hours in 1 day and/or over 40 hours worked in 1 week. Double time for Sundays and Double time plus normal holiday pay for working holidays.

73

- Add the requirement for apprentice experience to include "company proven experience and employee signed agreement" along with "DOL approved training class".

- Make 100% of all trade unions financial accounting available to union members and the Federal government upon request.

- Ensure that the government agency (Office of Labor Management Standards) responsible for investigating union business practices is fully funded.

Now these may seem like reasonable things to you and me, but I will explain why some will not like them and the arguments that unions and the politicians in their pocket will have.

1. Raising the $2,000 dollar limit to today's standards will limit the amount of work available to unions because Independent contractors would not have to follow the prevailing wage requirements that inflate costs to match union prices. So unions, unless they changed, would not be able to compete on projects under $28,000.00. Unions would object not because it is bad for the people, but because it would employ people that are not paying them dues.

2. Changing current 2 employee voting requirements to over 10 would limit unions' ability to eliminate or harass competition while companies are still small and weak.

3. Making harassment illegal for companies with 10 or less employees or employees that belong to other unions will limit harassment of smaller, weaker competition. Like I mentioned before, unions exist not for employees but to increase their own money and power. People in other unions are still their enemy. They will fight this issue by

claiming that their "freedom of speech" rights are being violated. But in truth they can complain all they want from afar, they just will not be able to do it in a way that disrupts business.

4. Fixing the prevailing wage will stop unions from inflating the prevailing wage to cover their exaggerated prices and excessive amounts for benefits.

5. Right now the way some prevailing wage laws read it could be possible if work hours were 3pm to 11:30pm that the employee would have to be paid overtime for all hours worked after 4:30pm even though they have only been at work for 1 ½ hours. This is a terrible waste of taxpayer money.

6. Currently the federal government states that anyone not in an approved DOL training class has to be paid Journeyman wages. It also states that you may only have (1) 3rd year apprentice and (1) apprentice of any year working with every (1) Journeymen. So if new hires or company trained people not in a DOL class are on the job they are classified as journeymen and have to be paid as journeymen. I believe that this was originally designed to drive up expenses for independent contractors. It would be much more efficient for employers to show work experience by DOL class or past work experience with employees signing off that they have no previous experience outside of the company or that they have provided records of all previous experience to the company in the form of past check stubs, etc.. Remember the goal here is not to show experience, but to prove that they have less experience so they can be paid less in correlation to their experience as per current DOL requirements. This allows for more

apprentice level positions to be filled by traditional hiring methods and reduces taxpayer cost.

7. If a union is supposedly established by its members and is there for its members then why shouldn't its members know where all of the union's money is going? Everyone else has to show the federal government their books, why shouldn't unions?

8. Since 2001, the Office of Labor Management Standards (OLMS) has assisted in securing 775 convictions of union officers and employees who "broke the law and betrayed the trust of their union members." Additionally, OLMS has assisted in recovering more than $70 million in union dues stolen by union officials, but their budget is always being cut.

In closing, I would like to say, President Obama the change everyone was looking for was not the change from Republican policy to Democrat policy.

But fixing that is for another book!

Acknowledgements

This information from (http://www.ij.org) was used with permission from the *Institute for Justice.*

Capitalism Magazine (http://www.capmag.com/)
Walter Williams' article in the December 2003 issue provided many of the quotations used regarding the 1931 passage of the Davis Bacon Act.

United States Department of Labor (http://www.dol.gov/)
This reference includes their many individual departments like the National Labor Relations Board (NLRB), Bureau of Labor Statistics, etc.

United States Chamber of Commerce (http://uschamber.com/)

OpenContracting (http://opencontracting.com/)

The Beacon Hill Institute (http://www.beaconhill.org/)

Associated Builders and Contractors, Inc. (http://www.abc.org/)

Independent Electrical Contractors (http://www.ieci.org/)

University of San Diego History Dept.
(http://history.sandiego.edu/gen/soc/labor-links.html)

Chicago-Kent College of Law and the *Illinois Labor History Society*
(http://www.kentlaw.edu/ilhs/curricul.htm#2)

McMahon

And several news agencies